Only the Ice Cream Shows

Rhyme with Reason

by
Sheror Caton Moore

Table of Contents

Life Is A Tapestry

Be Of Good Cheer, It Is I

Where I Am, God Is!

Introduction

God Has always used poetry to bring comfort to his people. Sheror Caton Moore has captured God's heart with this collection of original poems. You will laugh, you will cry, you will gain a new perspective on an intimate walk with God as you read *Only The Ice Cream Shows.*

~ Judith M. Lee

Rhyme with Reason

Only the Ice Cream Shows

There's something I want to state
about the problem of my weight.
I know that it's a sin
to let yourself get in the shape I'm in.
I'm going to control it – I can I know –
meanwhile I'm glad that my other sins don't show.

When I don't read my bible or pray –
or some angry word I say –
I'm so thankful people only see –
the french fries sagging on me.
And when I tell a little lie
it doesn't hang on my hips like apple pie.

I wonder how I'd look if each unkind thought
tightened around my knees like the pants I bought.
And whatever would I do to hide
my hate, if it hung outside
for all the world to see that sin –
hanging there like a double chin.

If my indifference stuck like glue –
the way Italian sausages do,
and if gossiping put fat where I once was thin –
oh my, what a shape I'd be in.
If every little doubt were a piece of lemon pie –
my weight scales could not measure that high.

Thank goodness that no one but God knows –
because when you look at me
                    only
                        the
                            ice cream
                                shows!

One More Night with the Frogs

In Exodus, Chapter Eight,
There's a story to relate.
When Moses came to the pharaoh
and said, "Let my people go.
Or God will bring frogs to your land
to cover everything by His mighty hand."

Pharaoh refused and the frogs came -
and he had no one but himself to blame.
So he called Moses to appear to him.
to see if God would get rid of them.
Moses agreed if his people would be free,
and asked Pharaoh when he wanted this to be.
Pharaoh said, "Tomorrow is a good day,
to get the frogs out of the way."

What he's saying there my mind just boggs!
Does he really want to spend another night
                          with the frogs?

I think with this story it's easy to see
how ridiculous we all tend to be.
The Lord is willing to clean up our life
and get rid of all the problems and strife.
But like old Pharaoh we want to spend one more night
                          in sin's filthy delight.
Instead of letting God's blessings come our way,
we put it off just one more day.

The "Diet Pepsi" Generation

The "Diet Pepsi Diet" is an easy one,
you eat everything you want and
                    when you're done,
just so your guilty conscious you can ease,
you smile and order "Diet Pepsi Please".

Sometimes in our Christian lives we go
                    with this plan,
to get by with all that we can.
Then when our conscious hurts and aches –
We ask God to forgive our 'mistakes'.

We sit down with Satan and we do as he wishes
we drink of his cup and eat off his dishes.
We fall for every little devilish tease
and finally say, "A little religion please".

Let's not fall for the easy way –
but let Jesus teach us each day.
And then we'll know the "Diet Pepsi Generation"
is just a pitiful imitation.

6

The Dream

God gave me a dream last night
that gave me marvelous insight.
I was lonely and poor just as I am today.
then a kind rich man came my way.

He wanted to marry me and make me his own –
and reign with him on his princely throne.
He was sending his limousine to my lowly door
to take me to live with him forevermore.

I sat about with great worry and strife –
to find just the right dress to present myself
                            To the love of my life.
I searched and searched and in my heart was great pain –
for all my clothing was ragged and worn and the
                            search was in vain.

The best that I had, myself to adorn –
was faded, ragged, and very worn.

But just as he promised he came and took me to
                            his palace on a high hill.
He asked, "Will you love and honor me?" I said, "I will."
Then love poured from him so tender and true –
that in my grateful heart I suddenly knew,
that the clothing he gave me was spun of pure gold –
and the love he gave would never grow old.

Isaiah 64:6
"...all our righteousnesses are as filthy rags..."

Tomorrow's Dream and Yesterday's Regret

I come to You, Lord, my heart beset –
between tomorrow's dream and yesterday's regret.

Don't let me dream so long that I fail to do
today's work that will honor You.

And Lord, don't let my regrets steal from me
TODAY'S OPPORTUNITY.

For that opportunity is <u>now</u> least I forget –
between tomorrow's dream and yesterday's regret.

Philippians 3:13
"I do forgetting those things which are behind, and reaching forth unto those things which are before."

Sunflowers

A sunflower turns its golden head
always toward the sun,
so it's been said.

Keeping the face
with beauty and grace
ever on that lightened place.

Lord, let me
forever be
a sunflower, too –
keeping my eyes on You.

Hidden Treasures

When God gave us earthly treasures, He placed them deep
inside the ground -
so that only by searching, could the glorious blessings be
found.
Then in His majestic power He has carefully designed
a place in our hearts given to the desire to find
all the great treasure - diamonds, silver and gold -
and given us eyes its beauty to behold.

But miracle of miracles, in our spiritual life,
He placed treasures deep inside the ground -
and only by seeking can the glorious treasures be found.
And in His majestic power He has carefully designed
a longing in our hearts with the desire to find
all the great treasures - faith, long suffering, hope, and love,
patience, kindness, joy - all treasures from our
Heavenly Father above.

Matthew 13:44
"Again, the kingdom of heaven is like treasure hidden in a field, which
when a man hath found, he hideth, and for joy of it goeth and selleth all
that he hath, and buyeth that field."

Free Indeed

Long ago when Rome was in its glory,
there comes a beautiful, sweet story.

A slave named Onesimus decided one day
that he would take his master's money and run away.

So he took his belongings and left his master's home,
and tried to hide himself in far-away Rome.

He met a man who was in prision, his name was Paul,
(before he met the Lord, his name was Saul).

Paul showed Onesimus the truth and the way,
and he asked Christ to come into his heart that day.

Onesimus felt he had to set things right,
so he left for his master's home that night.

With a letter from Paul so full of love,
it is written straight from the heart of God above.

"Philemon, please receive Onesimus, my beloved son,
whom I have begotten in my bonds.

"In times past he was not profitable to thee,
But now he is profitable to thee and me.

"He is now much more than a servant, beloved to me,
but how much more unto thee.

"If he has wronged thee or owes you any amount,
Put that on my account."

It is like my Savior saying with overwhelming love,
as He talks to the heavenly Father above.

Receive Sheror as Myself and if she owes any amount,
Just put the whole thing on My account!

Whom the Son sets free, is free indeed!

Book of Philemon

The Common Thread

From Genesis to Revelation there is a sweet common thread
A loving Heavenly Father desiring to restore that which
was dead.
Adam was a spirit man who walked with God –
and was given dominion over birds of the air, fish in the sea
and the ground he trod.
But he gave up his spiritual freedom and became a
creature of skin –
He reasoned with the mind instead of walking in the spirit,
thus the beginning of sin.

But God's loving spirit is Holy and true –
and He called out his people and began to woo –
He wooed them with the occupation of land,
for with the reasoning of the mind, that was all
they could understand.
And with understanding God wanted to restore
His chosen people to a spiritual walk of dominion once more.

His communion was broken time and time again
as He tried to fellowship with fallen man.
But God cannot dwell where there is sin –
and He knew there had to be a mediator
between Himself and men.
Yes, the only covering for the sins of everyone
was the precious Holy blood of Jesus His Son.

He placed His Holy blood in a body of flesh and feet of clay –
So that we, His people, would at last know the way
to walk in the spirit and have dominion once more –
Just as Adam did before.
This is the thread that runs Holy and true –
God's loving desire to dwell and commune with me and you

Seasons of Life

Lord, pierce our hearts with the words that
everything has its season
And it's not for us to know your reasons.
There's a time to be born, a time to die.
and ours not to question why.

A time to kill – a time to be healed,
A time to tear down and a time to build.

A time to laugh, a time to weep –
A time to cast away and a time to keep.

a time to lose and a time to gain –
A time to embrace and a time to refrain.

A time for war, a time Your peace to seek –
A time of silence, a time to speak.

Let us realize that Your time is perfect, and
in You will it bring,
Peace, love and understanding, in all things.

Ecclesiastes Chapter 3
1st Thessalonians 5:1

12

A Touch of Faith

"And His disciples said unto Him, Thou seest the
multitude thronging Thee, and sayest Thou, Who
touched Me?"

That question thrills and electrifies
when you come to realize
that the Savior who was thronged so much
was stopped by a nameless woman's touch.

Her name we do not know, she was just
a nameless face
in a noisy crowded eastern market place.
The crowd gets louder and many start to run
because they want to catch a glimpse of a certain
"Someone."

It is His face that will hold your gaze
and you will remember the rest of your days.
Once you've seen that face, you will see it everywhere.
Once you've heard that voice, you will hear it
in the air.

His name is Jesus from Galilee,
and it is His face that she longs to see.
With Him there is no more suffering or persecution.
No more hunger, death, or disillusion.

(He is on a mission to restore
a little girl to health once more.)

Now here she stands pale and wane
her face is streaked with pain.

There have been many tears
in her suffering that has lasted twelve years.
Her body is pain racked and drawn,
and each day is just another hopeless dawn.

The assurance came to her that special day
that if she could touch the hem of His garment as He
        passed her way,
that healing would be hers and she'd be whole again.
If... she could only touch the garment of this wonderful
        man.

With a trembling finger she managed to reach out,
Yes, she had touched His robe, there was no doubt.
Through her body the power began to flow
and she felt the vitality, a healthy glow.
She almost shouted out loud,
but she quietly sank into the crowd.

Then came the question that put her down in history,
the savior asked, "Who touched me?"
The crowd grew silent, there was hardly a stir,
and then His glance fell upon her.
He said the words that shook her very soul:
"Daughter, thy faith hath made thee whole."

The touch of a nameless woman stopped the
                        Lord of Eternity!
She touched Him.......and so can we!!

Mark 5:34
"And he said unto her, Daughter, thy faith hath made thee whole; go in
peace, and be whole of thy plague"

Inspired by a sermon of Dr. Peter Marshall

He Saved Others; Himself He Cannot Save

There He hung on that tree,
In a place called Calvary.

There was a dark strange cloud -
That caused uneasiness in the crowd.

There were fingers pointing to that cross so cruel,
Mocking fingers of scorn and ridicule.

There were also tears of men and women being shed -
Because they knew He was dying in their stead.

Peter stood at the crowd's edge, his very heart broken -
As he remembered the words of denial he had spoken.

The crowd roared, "Come down from the cross, that's what you can do.
Come down from the cross, then we will believe you.

You saved others, now Yourself You cannot save
And this day you'll surely go to your grave."

His Prayer was sure and true,
"Father, forgive them, for they know not what they do."

Then there was a victorious cry for all who chose to hear it,
"It is finished, Father, into Thy hands I commit My Spirit."

"He saved others: Himself He cannot save." They were wrong-yet right.
He could have called twelve legions of angels to rescue Him from this
plight.

But He was willing to pay the cost,
"I am come to seek and to save that which was lost."

The acorn cannot save itself, if it is to bud a tree;
The soldier cannot save himself, if he is to save his country.

The only way Christ could bring salvation for you and me
Was to give Himself willingly.

In order to right all the wrongs since the world began
He assumed all the sorrows and burdens of men,
And with a broken heart He died on that tree,
Because He couldn't save Himself - and save me.

Inspired by a sermon of Dr. Peter Marshall

The Promised Day of Pentecost

Disciples: I have always thought they were the elite
because they actually sat at His feet.
The parables they heard Him teach
and they sat under trees and heard Him preach.
They saw His miracles and walked with Him.
And for these reasons I've envied them.

Yet when Jesus was arrested they ran away.
I've always wondered if they had feet of clay.
I've often thought how brave I'd be.
If only I'd had their opportunity.

How did they walk with Him three years
share His laughter and His tears
and not be changed through and through?
Didn't they know there was a job to do?

What did it take to change them?
Not the crucifixion nor the resurrection of Him!
But just when they thought all was lost
came the promised day of Pentecost.

Not until they were filled with the Holy Spirit that
day
were they changed in every way.
Not until then did they see the meaning clear
not until then did bravery replace fear.

So therein lies our blessed hope
in the darkness we won't have to grope.
And even though we didn't walk with Him
He sends the same Holy Spirit that He sent them.

The Rock That Moved

It is in mysterious and different ways
that God brings back memories of other days.
To some it could be a certain song
or a picture that's been stored so long.
Memories... They come surging back
either to heal or accuse and attack.

To Simon Peter, who was called "The Rock"
it was the simple crowing of the cock.
When the murmuring voices faded away
     into the night
he fought a gripping fear with all his might.
The realization came that Jesus was marching
     away to die
and that the dreaded time was drawing nigh.

Jesus had told him, "Before the cock crows and
     dawn we see
three times, Peter, you will deny me."
First to the girl at the Palace door
also to the soldier he denied Him once more.
Then to another soldier he cursed and
     swore again,
"I know not this man."

Then far off in the distance he heard
      the cock crow.
He wanted to run but there was no place to go.
He remembered what the Lord had said,
with hot tears streaming, he wished he were dead.

But, let's not leave Peter here
a traitor, broken with fear.
That would not be fair to him in this undertaking
because this apostle is still in the making.

Jesus had told him, "I prayed that your faith will
      fail not."
So there's still a job for him, but what?
He carried so much guilt and self-blame
that all he could do was nurse his deep shame.

He tried to put away sorrow and all regrets
and went back to his fishing nets.
One night while fishing he looked on shore
and there he saw his Savior once more.
His repentance and pledge of love was deep
and the Lord said to him, "Feed my sheep."
Healed and converted and forgiven of sin
he is now ready for his powerful ministry to
      begin.

Inspired by a sermon of Dr. Peter Marshall

Disciples

What if Jesus had asked us one day
to help him pick disciples to follow His way?
If we had examined all of them
we'd likely find them unworthy to follow Him.

The first candidate is coming up from the beach
his boat he just pulled on shore with
    a strong reach.
His hands are calloused, he smells of fish, too.
Just what ministering job could he do?
He is stubborn and set in his ways
and he's been a fisherman all his days.

Simon doesn't seem to be material for
    the ministry.

The next candidates are brothers who
    are fishermen too.
They can forecast weather by looking at the sky
and when it comes to fishing – they are sly.
They are very boastful which earned them some
    local fame,
'Sons of thunder' is their nickname.

James and John are just too loud; they will not do.

The next candidate has a gleam in his eyes
he's the fanatical type that most people despise.

He dreams of the day the kingdom will be
    restored,
and has malice in his heart that he can ill afford.

No, Judas is too impatient...

Here comes another fisherman on the scene,
He is neither gentle nor mean.
He is cautious and demands proof of everything.
Delay to the group is all he can bring.

No, Thomas is too cautious.

The next man has a calculating mind –
that is quite devious we find.
A tax collector by trade,
many enemies he has made.
He has a passion for family trees,
and will bore you with recitals of best families.

No, Matthew must be rejected.

What about Andrew and Bartholomew,
Thaddeus, Phillip and James – will they do?
Not hardly by our standards today
we would probably turn them away.

But Jesus chose them because He could see
not what they were, but what they could be.

Inspired by a sermon of Dr. Peter Marshall

Eternity
In
My
Heart

Eternity in My Heart

Deep in the heart of me
God has placed eternity.
In that Holy place
He has dropped peace and grace.
He has given me love and serenity –
For in my heart is God's eternity.

In His glorious plan there is always a reason –
and in His time everything is beautiful in
                                    its season.
Whatever God does, forever shall be –
so he places in our hearts all eternity.

What has already been – will be again.

There is nothing new under the sun –
what will be has already been done.
This is the comfort my heavenly father
                                    gives to me –
as He places in my heart all eternity.

Ecclesiastes 3:11-14
"He hath made every thing beautiful in his time: also he hath set the world
in their heart, so that no man can find out the work that God maketh from
the beginning to the end"

God Has No Calendar

God has no calendar; we need always to understand –
A day to Him is but a footprint in life's eternal sand.
For a brief moment there's an indentation only to be
    swept away –
It's here, then 'tis gone, except in our remembrance
                    - A Golden Day.

His timing is perfect, though to us it may seem –
that tomorrow is forever an unrealized dream.
But to GOD yesterday and tomorrow are just the same
    as today
And the prayers and dreams we've hoped for are just –
                A breath away.

Galatians 4:10
"Ye observe days, and months, and times, and years."

Sin

I have seen sin, in my life and in that of others;
I've seen it separate families and break the heart
of mothers.
I've seen it turn father against son
and tear down relationships one by one.

The devil will have you begin
by indulging in one little sin.
And before you know what's happened to you
that sin will be all you want to do.
It will take you down roads you never dreamed
you'd go
It will teach you things you didn't want to know.
Your life will be filled with confusion and fear.
You'll never even think of the Savior so dear.

Three things about sin I want you to know.
It will take you further than you want to go.
It will keep you longer than you want to stay.
It will cost more than you want to pay.

So if you will live happy and free
from sin you should always flee.
when you feel it slipping in
Ask Jesus to forgive that sin.

The Brook That Ran Dry

"As the Lord God of Israel lives before Whom I stand,"
Elijah prayed, "there will be no dew or rain in the land."

Get away from here and go to the Cherith brook;
So he drank, and food from the raven he partook.

After awhile the brook completely dried
and food from the ravens was denied.

Then God sent Elijah to the widow's house to sustain him -
and there he multiplied the meal and oil for them.

Now why, why, WHY - would God send him
to a brook that ran dry?

Why did He send him to a widow who had not enough for
herself
of meal in the kitchen bin nor oil on the kitchen shelf?

Because God wanted to teach Elijah the same thing
He wants to teach me today.
To have enough faith to walk in His Way.

Sometimes we drink from a little cup
when God sends us to a brook and it dries up.

Faith is hard when the human eye wants to see
the secret work God does in you and in me.

1 Kings 17:4
"And it shall be, that thou shalt drink of the brook; and I have commanded
the ravens to feed thee there."

Winds of Change

Behold, a new thing, Lord I want to see it,

Not with physical eyes –

But with the eyes of the Spirit.

And with my Spiritual ears –

I can hear it.

It is the sound of moving waters –

And the wind of change.

God wants to set in order and be given permission

To rearrange.

Taking away old things that are out-dated

And out of season.

Teaching me to "let go" without questioning

His Divine reason.

Just as in days of old when on the wilderness journey –

God's cloud overhead –

Would move and He guided His people –

Just as he said.

Lord, when I sense your cloud is moving –

Let my heart be at rest.

Let me lay down your good thing and

Reach our for your best

Isaiah 43:18-19
"Remember ye not the former things, neither consider the things of old.
Behold, I will do a new thing; now it shall spring forth;
shall ye not know it?"

A Prayer in Fall

Lord,
The leaves are changing –
It is the glorious Fall season –
Lord, is that the reason –
My spirit is crying out for change too?
For that glorious change that comes
only from you.

I know, dear Heavenly Father, with the turning
of the leaves
There is a death, too.
But only in death are you able to bring the new.

Lord, you have made the season of dying to be
such a colorful, beautiful thing.
That with its memory we can face Winter
and with joyful anticipation
Look forward to Spring.

Promises in Psalm 37

We are not to fret over evildoers
        That is the command from the start
We are to trust the Lord and dwell in the
        land and He will give us the desires of our heart.

We are to trust in the Lord and He will bring our
        rightousness to pass in a wonderful way -
And our justice will shine as noon day.

Lord, let us cease from anger and in Your love rest
For only then can we be truly blessed.

Greater is the little of a righteous man
Than the riches of the wicked who scour the land

In the days of famine the upright shall be
        satisfied and not be ashamed.
But the wicked, like the splendor of the meadows
        shall vanish and be defamed.

The steps of a good man are ordered of God.
        Though He falls the Lord holds Him
                        with His hand.
For the good man delights in the way of the
        Lord's command.

His descendants are blessed and
                their descendants after them
For the Lord is faithful to bless those who seek
        and follow him.

Back To The Cross

Point me back to the cross, Lord, show me the
   way,
For only from the view of the cross can I look
   forward to today.
When I look back and realize the sacrifice You
   gave for me –
Then my spirit will be lifted and be totally free.

Adam's blood pumped through my veins and was
   leading me to the grave –
Until I was covered by God's blood that you gave.
Now I am a new creation with Your Holy blood
   flowing through me –
And, now, instead of death and defeat I have
   Your victory.

So point my spirit eyes back to the cross, Lord,
   allow me to see –
The victorious seed of Your blood that was passed
   down to me.

Praise the Lord!

A Proverb

The mouth of the righteous speaks wisdom
and none of his steps shall slide.

For the law of the Lord is in his heart
and in his heart
truth shall ever abide.

If we wait on the Lord
and keep His way,
the wicked world that judges us
will pass away.

The salvation of the righteous
is from the Lord
and He will deliver them.

Because they **Trust in Him**!

Amen

Proverbs 8:8a
"All the words of my mouth are in righteousness"

A Pot Called Romans 8:28

I have a great big pot - its name is Romans
8:28 -
So when I think God is running late -
with a prayer that needs an answer and
cannot wait -
I simply place it in my pot called Romans
8:28

He is working it all together for my good -
And things would go better if I only would.
Put it in my pot called Romans 8:28
And know God is never too early nor too
late -
He's just working it all for good while I
wait.

With the lid closed tight on my pot called
Romans 8:28.

*"And we know that all things work together for good to them that love God,
to them who are the called according to his purpose."*

The Visitor

It was an ordinary Sunday morning like
                    many, many before,
But as the little choir was singing, a stranger walked
                    through the door.
Suddenly the singing took on a heavenly tone -
and the music was sweeter and clearer than
                    we had ever known.

The message had new depth and height and meaning
            as it fell on that small congregation,
And each heart was stirred to a
            fresh exciting palpitation.

The Visitor silently slipped away.

There was no sound of a car nor shuffle of feet,
we ran outside, but there was no one on the street.

Our hearts yearned for fellowship with the stranger so
                    fair,
And somehow we knew we had entertained an Angel
                    unaware.

I'll never forget that Sunday morning though time
                    travels on through space.
That beautiful Sunday morning when I looked upon
                    His wonderful face.

Matthew 5:8
"Blessed are the pure in heart, for they shall see God."

Soldiers on a Battlefield

Soldiers on a battlefield –

 but the battle has already been won;

Soldiers who can't realize –

 It is finished, totally done.

Soldiers that know no other way –

 But to go out and fight Satan each day.

Soldiers who have never known peace –

 So their minds cannot conceive –

The things that are in their hearts –

 That they want desperately to believe.

So they just keep fighting battles –

 In themselves they cannot win –

And overlook God's love gift – peace within.

1 John 5:4,5
"For whatever is born of God overcomes the world. And this is the victory
that has overcome the world – our faith. Who is he who overcomes the
world, but he who believes that Jesus is the Son of God?"

The Opposite of Faith

Have faith, even in a world of greed,
Have faith, that God will attend every
                              need.
His gentle hand will lead us to pastures
                              green,
and give us things hoped for - yet unseen.
"Have Faith," His gentle words we hear,
The opposite of faith is not doubt, but fear.

We're afraid that in this world of greed,
that God doesn't even know our need.
We're afraid to hope for things unseen -
and afraid our pastures won't be green.
Fear - what a sin to His Holy Name -
Lord, forgive me, now faith I claim.

1 John 4:18
"perfect love casteth out fear."

The Perfect Church

I am really in a lurch –
looking for the perfect church.
One where the Spirit is free –
and love flows endlessly.
I wonder where it can be.

In this perfect place
the preacher will have a gentle face.
Yet will be firm in a way –
and will always know just what to say
to brighten the dreary day.

The preacher's partner for life
will be the perfect preacher's wife.
She will play the piano and teach – and be in charge of outreach –
and listen attentively to every word preached.

The choir will sing in perfect pitch –
and get along without a hitch.
They will never quabble over who sings best –
and one won't try to outdo the rest.
They will come to practice with enthusiasm and zest.

This perfect church I'll never find –
for it is only in my poor mind.
People make up churches so they're imperfect – still,
I wonder if I ever will
find a church that is REAL!!!

The Knower and The Doer

The doer said to the knower one day,
*   "What's with you?*
All for you is to be, and I have to rush
*   around and do?*

You have much peace, and your burdens
*   seem so light,*
I have so many activities that I work
*   day and night.*

The harder I work the greater the strain –
and I'm left with, not joy, but sorrow and pain.

The work that you do seems to bring you such rest,
while I work and work for relief from the test."

Said the knower to the doer, "My words are true –
if you knew with your knower, your doer
*   wouldn't have to do."*

Matthew 11:28
"Come unto me all ye that are heavy laden – I will give you rest."

If I Were The Devil

If I were the Devil,
let me tell you what I would do –
I'd make salvation look complicated
so it would confuse you.
I'd convince you that you're alright
with your 'sinful life style',
And smile to myself all the while.

I'd let you blame others
 during trouble and strife,
so you wouldn't know it was me
destroying your life.
I'd convince you right is wrong
and wrong is right,
I wouldn't be lazy; I'd work day and night.

While you slept I'd take your freedoms
one by one –
and I would never sleep until
all this was done.

YOU KNOW WHAT?
THAT IS JUST WHAT HE DOES!!

Grandmother's Quilts

Grandmother was a simple Person –
frills just were not her style.
She enjoyed the simple pleasures –
like a child's warm smile.
The quilts she made were not fancily designed,
they were made with one purpose in mind.
to keep out the cold chilly bite –
of a winter's frosty night.
I remember those old patch work quilts so well –
Scraps of dresses my mother wore,
little pieces of my own pinafore.
Bits of my brother's shirts showed up
                            here and there –
sewn together with patience and care.
It was so cozy to settle down –
with little memories of my loved ones all around.
with love each quilt had been hand sewn,
Yes, Grandmother had a style all her own.

In memory of Grandmother – Alice Caton

Like a Flood

When the enemy comes in, the Lord says it's "like a flood."
There is destruction, devastation, and mud.
The houses that were once lighted and shown beautiful,
                                        sparkling clean,
Are covered with muddy waters and can't even be seen.

Ugly devastation is all around –
Then the snakes are washed up out of the ground.
The snakes of disappointment, pain, and strife,
Put dread, anger, and fear in our life.

But, Lord, You said when the enemy comes in like an
                                        old earthly flood,
That you would lift a banner out of the mire and mud.
That banner is our Lord Jesus, and when we look upon
                                        His face,
              By His Love and Power and Grace,

We are lifted above the devastation and pain
Higher and higher to a heavenly plain,
Where snakes and destruction can never reign.

Thank you, Lord, for Your promise divine;
I praise Your Holy Name that this promise is mine!

Hallelujah!!

Isaiah 59:19
"When the enemy shall come in like a flood, the Spirit of the LORD shall lift
up a standard against him."

The First Stone

In John, Chapter 8, there's a wonderful example
    for us to see –
A woman was brought to Jesus who had been
    caught in adultery.
The law in this case was clear as could be –
Death by stoning was the penalty.

But Jesus had an answer that was uniquely
    His own –
"Let he who is without sin cast the first stone."
So dear brothers and sisters when you become
    perfect in every way –
Here is your stone you can cast at some poor
    sinner some day!

(Until then... just keep it as a reminder!)

John 8:7
*"So when they continued asking him, he lifted up himself, and said unto
them, He that is without sin among you, let him first cast a stone at her."*

Noble Wife

Lord, did the lady in
       Proverbs 31
ever have any fun?

I know she got up before
       day light
and worked hard 'til late
       at night.
     By candlelight.

She was also in Real Estate –
She considers fields while her husband
       sits at the gate.

She is not concerned about snow
    because she has taken time
       out to sew,
making her family warm clothes –
     wouldn't you know!

And, on top of that, she sews so well,
that in her spare time she makes sashes
       to sell!!!

I realize that charm is deceitful
    and beauty is vain,
but I wonder if she might be
      a little plain.
Apparently she's not one to complain.

Her own works give her praise –
    all her days –

Still, her life seemed a little rough –
   I guess praise was enough.

Life
Is
A
Tapestry

Life is a Tapestry

Life is a tapestry being woven by God's own hand.
He carefully and lovingly chooses each colored strand.
Each day is a thread in the pattern that He has
                              planned carefully –
And only He knows what the design
                              of each tapestry will be.

The ordinary days are the background,
        and suddenly there appears
        the vibrant colors of God-dried tears,
        surrendered disappointments and fears

The colors of the love we share –
Are woven in with tender care.

The beautiful pattern is set ablaze –
As we give the Great Weaver our joy and praise.

Disappointment comes when our view of the pattern
                              looks vague
and the storms of life are at high tide.
And we can't seem to realize that God sees His
wonderful creations from the other side.

Clean Windows

I looked out my window
    and saw my neighbor's clothes
        hanging on her line...
They were dingy and dirty looking
    not nearly as clean as mine.
I felt so sorry for her in my
    self-righteous little way,
How awful it must be
    to hang them out
    day after day,
For all the world to see –
Oh, how embarrassing that must be.

I decided one day to wash my
windows to a clean bright shine –
Lo and behold, her laundry
    looked cleaner than mine.

Matthew 7:3
"And why beholdest thou the mote that is in thy brother's eye, but
considerest not the beam that is in thine own eye?"

A Christian's Disney World

Sometimes the servants of God get caught up in a whirl -
in what is like a Christian's Disney World.
Some walk the streets of Frontier Land,
where the past is lived forever at their command.
They cannot shake the memory of things they have done,
they cannot accept the forgiveness of God's Son.

Some follow the colorful marching band,
into the dreams of Tomorrow Land.
They live their lives with their minds on what will be -
today's opportunities their eyes never see.

Others travel in Fantasy Land where everything is small -
and the giant problems of life seem only two feet tall.
With their head in a cloud, they wonder around -
their feet somehow never touch the ground.

Lastly there's the pilgrims in Adventure Land -
where there's excitement on every hand.
The miracles they've experienced make them want to stay
and they forget about their brother who has lost his way.

What we Christians need to do -
is realize what is false and true.
Let's not get caught up in the make believe whirl -
of the many lands of a Christian's Disney World.

He is Always There

God never closes the door that we open with prayer.

He is always listening to us and waiting –

      our burdens to bear.

We need to confess our sins and be thankful His mercies

      are new each day,

so we can start fresh and carry no 'baggage' along our way.

the greatest and most awesome call on our lives

      is to converse

with the wonderful, great God of the Universe.

It is our very life and breath,

and has called us to life from death.

When we are alone with God in the secret place.

There alone will we see His Holy face.

It reveals the false from the true –

and the knotted tangled mess of our life He will undo.

He gives us the answers that only He,

         in His wisdom, knows –

And we find cleansing and rest for our weary souls.

God rocks the world with the simplest prayer –

This thought rocks my world – I can enter the Throne-room

AND HE IS ALWAYS THERE.

Fast Then Feast

Fast from judging others –
Feast on Christ dwelling in them.
Fast from fear of illness –
Feast on the Healing power of God.
Fast from words that hurt –
Feast on words that purify
and edify.
Fast on problems –
Feast on prayer that sustains.
Fast on discontent –
Feast on Gratitude.
Fast on anger –
Feast on thankfulness.
Fast on gossip-
Feast on silence.
Fast on worry –
FEAST ON HIM.

The Rejected Stone

Michelangelo saw a stone one day
That many had rejected along the way
Perhaps it was because they could not see
The beauty of the finished product
that would be.
Michelangelo, however, saw things that
no one else could.
And already knew that the figure he
sculpted would be lovely and good.
It was that very day he saw in that
piece of marble the tender smile
of mother Mary holding the beautiful
Jesus child.
Oh, Lord, how wonderful it is to know that
you look at this old lump of clay
And see the awesome work of art the
finished product will be someday.

Glory Clouds

In nature, Lord, you show us the spiritual things
    as well.
You use the wonders around us Your secrets to
    tell.

The sun draws water and gathers it in a cloud on
    high.
Then at the proper time - rains it back down on
    the earth from the sky.

As for our prayers, Lord, the same is true.
The tears, the praise, the worship is drawn back to
    You.

You gather them in a glory cloud on high
And at the proper time You rain down
Your blessings from the heavenly sky.

A Kiss From The Groom

There were hundreds in the congregation
that morning
    We were in one heart.

Our purpose was to praise Him,
    and lift His name on high.

The unity of our love for Him
    turned into worship

The heavenly choir of angels soon
    joined in.

Time stood still as adoration
    flowed.

Then the glorious fragrance of heaven
    filled the room.

The bride had received a wondrous
    kiss from the GROOM.

52

Born To Praise

The little songbird knows the true value of praise.
For that is the way she starts each of her days.
The worm in the ground –
feels the vibrations of that sound.
He wriggles his way top-side
and in this way the Lord Provides
Food for the song bird that was created to spend her days
giving God Almighty glory and praise

Psalm 150:6
"Let every thing that hath breath praise the Lord"

Exodus 15:2
"The Lord is my strength and song, and He is become my salvation: He is my God, and I will prepare Him an habitation"

Dear God,
I've been on the Mountain-top
and Your wonders I've been shown.
But, Sweet Jesus, You taught me
that it is in the valley that the fruit is grown.

Psalm 23:4
Yea, though I walk through the valley of the shadow of death, I will fear no evil; for Thou are with me; Thy rod and Thy staff they comfort me.

A Prayer - A Gift

Today, Lord, I saw upon the hill-
A glorious host of daffodils.
A little gift from You to me,
A fragrant promise for me to see.

The dreary winter is in my heart today -
But in my spirit the newness of spring is not far away.

Thank you, Lord, that the cold winter will soon be past -
And the fresh breeze of spring will lighten my heart at last

Thank you, Lord, for the assurance that is mine -
And for slowly revealing Your plan divine.
I thank You that I walk in the pathway clearly marked for me -
And the guiding light of Your love is all I need to see.

~~~~~~~~~~~~~~~~~~~~~~~~~

Dear Lord,

I've come to the end of myself once more -
I'm knelt before still another closed door.
I've struggled with circumstances and fought with pain -
Only to discover again, it is all in vain.

I have prayed and the heavens have been closed to me,
I have turned my faith eyes toward things I see.
I have trusted myself to know Your will in my life -
and that self trust has brought destruction and strife.

So I lay it down on the altar, Lord, the heartache and despair-
knowing and trusting that You are always there,
to pick up the broken pieces and make me whole again -
and give me joy in Your mercy.

Amen and Amen.

The Stranger's Story

It was hard for me to understand on that dreary day
Why our friends had suddenly turned away.
Then my darling husband whispered in my ear
Beautiful words I needed to hear.
"I love you now and I always will,
If the world turned against you I'd love you still."
We had been married for such a long time,
And a beautiful thought came to my heart-mind.
That when the Lord decided to call one of us home -
The other would just go too, and we'd never be alone.
I dared not speak the thought aloud -
It was there - then it disappeared like a puffy white cloud.

But God heard.

A few days later in our store a stranger walked in -
His face almost glowed with the warmest grin.
"You remind me of my father and mother -
You seem to have so much love for each other."
"May I," inquired he, "tell a story to you?
I somehow feel it will bless you two.
My daddy was a preacher and early in his life -
He asked the Lord to give him a good wife.
They served the Lord together, in servanthood ministry
He preached and she made chicken soup and tea.

That soup was anointed because she prayed as the pot
        steamed,
And while she prayed the Holy Spirit on her face gleamed.
She and daddy would take it to sick folk far and near -
Spreading the gospel and healing with chicken soup and
        God's cheer.

They served the Lord together for many a Blessed day –
Then came the time – the Lord decided to take Daddy away.

That night my sweet mama told all her sons goodbye,
She knew the time had come for her too – to go sailing
        through the sky.
The next day at the funeral mama lifted her hands to pray –
And went home to be with the Lord on that very day.

Yes, it is my prayer for you that you will be like my father
        and mother.
That you will serve the Lord and live for Him in love with
        each other.
And when the time comes a long time from now
You two will make the journey together somehow."

I dried tears from my eyes and looked up to find him gone
Was he an angel or a man? There was no way for me to
        have known.

But God knows –

Two years later I would look back on the story true –
And claim the promise from God for a long life for me and
        you.
That we would live for the Lord in love with each other –
And go together to our reward just like the stranger's father
        and mother.

Hebrews 13:2
"… thereby some have entertained angels unawares"

Written for my husband, Obie R. Moore, December 19, 1997, when he was
diagnosed with cancer.
He went home to be with the Lord August 28, 2006.

Lord,

If he is in heaven with You,
And You are in earth within me -
Then, Lord, where is He?

He lives in my heart -
And we are never apart...
I see his sweet smile in every twinkle of a star -
It gives my grieving heart comfort to know that he is where You
are.

And not far away - but close as can be -
Because he is with You -
And You are living in me...

In memory of my husband Obie R. Moore

Thy Kingdom Come - In Earth As It Is In Heaven!

Lord,
Help me -
　　　To see -

Your Kingdom,
　　　with Spiritual eyes -
　　　As my heart cries -

For More of You, and Less of Me -
　　　For, Lord, You said in Your word -
　　　And my Spiritual ears have heard -

That If My Heart Is Pure,
　　　I will be sure to see -
　　　YOU, in Your Great Majesty.

My Mother / My Little Girl

She's a child again and at long last
Gone are the stress and worry lines
                    from her past –
Gone are the memories of a childhood filled with
                    insecurity and fear –
Dim and distant are the eyes that were once
                    bright and clear.

Lord give me the strength that only comes
                    from above...
To give her this childhood filled with Your love.

What a happy child she is today –
Lord could she just stay this way?

She awakes each morning in a new world,
She picks flowers and gets her hair curled.
She's lost some things, but so what?
She laughs and giggles a lot.

*Written while caring for my mother, Mary Caton Boyer,
who passed away with Alzheimer's on June, 16, 1999*

Angels With White Puffy Wings

Today my little girl/mother and I-
Sat on the porch and watched puffy white clouds go by

One looked like a cat with its ears standing up -
One looked like a tin cup -

Still another looked like an angel with wings -
It was with wonderment that she saw all these things.

I was reminded of long ago -
When it was my finger pointing up with face aglow.

"I see an Angel. See the white puffy wings?"
I remembered - and it was the sweetest, saddest thing.

She walked out of the
fog today -
Long enough to pick
a fragrant rose bouquet -
And gave it away -
to a friend.

Living in the Past

She just sits there now, looking so alone
And I marvel at how wispy she's grown.
I can almost see her wasting away
Getting more frail every day.

She is in a little world of her own
Reliving the happy days she's known.
Living in the past and caring little for today
And that aggravates us in a strange way.

We yearn to have her as she was before.
We want her to have enthusiasm once more.
We want her to look for tomorrow
And not live in the past with its joy and its
                                          sorrow.

But her vivid memories could just be God's way
Of giving her the courage to face today.
Her life, long ago, was placed in His hands
And He knows and lovingly understands.

So, Lord, let us sincerely pray
For Your guidance every day.
And give us the wisdom to know
How to care for this "child" You love so.

Dear Lord,

Isn't she a delight?
     You made her that way.
She brought joy and beauty
     to every single day.
Don't let me morn for her
     or walk around with a long face.
But let me rejoice that she
     is finally in the right place.
She served You daily, Lord and
     I'm sure her mansion will be the one
That has a little flower garden
     in a little patch of sun.
Each flower that blooms will remind her
     of ones she left here.
And each morning as she walks
     she'll think of each one so dear
Heaven is beautiful, Lord, but
     I'm sure you'll let her know
That she can have her garden in heaven
     and watch lovely flowers grow.
Flowers such as have never been seen
     here on earth with human eye.
Flowers that won't need light
     or rain from the sky.
But flowers that bloom because
     she wishes it so.
She'll love it, Lord
     don't You just know!
Thank You, Lord, for the Christian
     life that she led.
And thank You, Lord, that I am one little flower
     in her flower bed.

Clouds May Come

Clouds do come, oh Lord, in grief I know,
Casting the seas of our lives to and fro...

But the rain that falls from the Almighty's
Hand -
Purges and heals a broken dry land.

Oh Lord, let this be -
Also in me -

For now I see through the cloud darkly,
But I trust You to keep me in Your Heart's
safe place -
And I will understand fully someday
When I see Your Glory face to face.

1 Corinthians 13:12
"For now we see through a glass, darkly; but then face to face"

Be Of Good Cheer,

IT IS I

64

Turkeys and Eagles

Once there were two eagles who
built a nest -
And were blessed with two
babies.

But in due season -
For some strange reason -

The parents left, never to return
And for food the babies began to
yearn.

They walked out on the cliff and
in great attempt tried to fly
From their safe home high in the
sky.

They flapped their wings as they
tumbled down -
But all attempts failed as they hit
the ground.

Just as they landed a turkey
passed their way -
And invited them into their flock
to stay.

Feeling totally accepted they
wanted to act like their new
found family -
So they copied everything they
did totally.

They even ate acorns that were
found under the tree.

But soon the two eagles found
They were not satisfied living on
the ground.

They looked up in the sky and
saw

Something they'd never seen
before -
Birds with wings outstretched -
And oh, how they wanted to soar.

"Don't ever think," the old turkey
said -
In a voice that was monotone
and flat -
"That you could ever soar like
that.

Don't think for a moment that
you could ever be
Soaring in Heavenly places
Happy and free.
No, you poor ugly turkeys, it's
just not meant to be."

So the eagles tried to be happy -
Oh, how hard they tried.
But there was just something
Deep down inside -

That made them want to just
give it a try -
As they watched the glorious
birds high in the sky.

One wonderful day while sitting
in a high tree
They stretched out their wings
and soared free.

They knew instantly
What God has purposed them to
be.

Free

Free

Free

Prayer On The Wings Of a Paper Eagle

On the wings of a paper eagle
    I wrote
        a note
            to You -
For, Lord, it was all that
    was left for me to do -
With the pain,
    the bitterness,
        the anger,
           the fears
The disappointment,
    the shattered dreams,
      and tears
And the unforgiveness I held onto for years.
On a paper eagle with all
    the faith my inner soul
      could bring -
I wrote and I wept and tied
    it to a balloon
      with a golden string.
I walked outside with a prayer
    for Your strength to show -
And with Your strength, praise God,
    I let it go.
What joy and peace filled my heart
    as I watched the balloon
      in the Heavenlies above -
A majestic golden eagle circled it -
    and electrified the air with the power
      of your love.

           Oh, Praise You God!

Isaiah 40:31
But they that wait upon the LORD shall renew their strength: they shall mount up with
wings as eagles

Deuteronomy 32:11, 12

Lord,

How does the eagle know when the time is right to stir up its nest? Except that your Holy Spirit move upon her and whisper in her ear:
   "It's time."
     "It's time."
       "It's time."

When her listening heart hears the whisper, she begins the task of stirring up the nest where her young ones have been at rest.

She plucks away the feathers that made their beds, soft and warm, and tosses them in the wind, until the prickly thorns are all that is left. The thorns that had held the soft fluffy feathers in place. That's all – all comfort is gone.

After she finishes this deliberate act of stirring up – she, of course, is not through. She lifts the eaglettes up, one by one, and pushes them over the high, high ledge. The first one tumbles, further, further, toward the ground. And just when he thinks it's over – she glides underneath her beloved youngster and lifts him onto her wing and gives him a glorious ride back to the safety of the ledge.

Then, she starts the process again, and again, and again. Until with great love and patience she has taught each one how to soar.

Oh father, let my heart hear your whisper,
        "It's time."
      "It's time."
     "It's time."

Rest From Fishing

I was walking on the beach one morning as the sun
                        was welcoming a new day.
I had come to a place of rest and stopped there to pray.

In the distance on the shore by the sea –
I saw a daddy with his son at his knee.

The daddy would cast his hook into the rolling tide –
The little boy would do the same right by his side.

The daddy would carefully show the little boy just
                        what to do –
There was great love and tenderness flowing between
                        the two.

After a long while the daddy sat down to rest there
                        by the beautiful sea,
And beckoned the little boy to come
                        and sit on his knee.

Thank You, Lord, for letting me see –
That is the kind of daddy you are to me.

Romans 8:15
"For ye have not received the spirit of bondage again to fear; but ye have
received the Spirit of adoption, whereby we cry, Abba, Father."

Fear Not, It Is I

After He fed the five thousand,
the disciples with Him wanted to abide.
But He constrained them in their ship,
and sent them to Jordan's other side.
And when He sent them away,
He departed to a mountain to pray.

They were in the midst of the sea and He saw
them rowing,
for the wind was contrary and strongly blowing.
He came walking on the water
and almost passed them by.
And then He heard their fearful cry.
gently to them He bade,
It is I, be not afraid.

How many times does He walk by;
and we are afraid to cry?
Cry out to the One who can still the sea;
Cry out for Him to calm the storm in you and me.
What a blessing when the storm is nigh,
to hear His sweet voice say, "Fear not, it is I."

Mark 6:50
"For they all saw him, and were troubled. And immediately he talked with
them, and saith unto them, Be of good cheer: it is I; be not afraid."

Fishers of Men

So many of the disciples were fishermen –
     I've oft wondered why.
Is it because a fisherman learns to read the signs
     of water and sky?
A true fisherman has the unique ability
to know where the fish are,
     by looking at the sky and sea.

He also has a talent that seems to be innate –
of knowing which fish will latch on to
          the proper bait.
He's not afraid of hard work,
         for the hours are long –
and the raw elements he daily lives with make
         him very strong.

Jesus knew those very qualities
would give them the strength for their ministries.
So he called them out, with a 'follow Me.'
     He forgave them of sin
and with the universal bait of love,
     He said, "I'll make you Fishers of Men."

Matthew 4:19
"And he saith unto them, Follow me, and I will make you fishers of men."

An Unknown Sea

Lord, my heart is almost shipwrecked as I come
    weakly to Your throne.
I've set sail on a sea that to me is virtually
    unknown.
The waves have tossed me to and fro - taking me
    further away from the land that I know.
The wind comes from strange directions playing
    havoc with my mind -
and my soul yearns for the peaceful shore now left
    so far behind.

But the sun in the east chases away darkness with
    its orange flame -
It enlightens my fearful heart as I call on Your
    Name.
Then deep in my troubled spirit, Lord, the
    assurance comes to me -
that new land cannot be discovered unless we set
    sail on an unknown sea.

Unknown Sea Prayer

Lord,

When I set my sail on the Unknown Sea,
I could not have guessed the plan You had for me.
I only knew –
That the winds of the Holy Spirit blew.
And guided my ship through –
Storms that I thought would destroy –
My faith, my hope, and my Joy –

IN YOU.

But as the voyage continued on that Unknown Sea –
You slowly revealed Your Glorious Plan for me.
And, at long last I knew –
That the only thing that I had to do –
Is keep my sail pointed up and the Wind of Your Spirit
will guide me through –
Any storm that would come to destroy –
My faith, my hope and my Joy ---

IN YOU.

Then at the end of my voyage on that Unknown Sea –
I can look back and rejoice at the awesome plan You had
for me.
And how wonderful it was that Your Holy Spirit blew –
To navigate my tiny ship through –
The uncharted waters – until the Promised Land came
into view.
And all the storms that I thought were to destroy –
Came from Your loving hand to strengthen my faith, my
hope and my everlasting joy ---

IN YOU.

Where I am,

God Is

Where I Am, God Is!

The light of God surrounds me
so the pathway I might see.

The love of God enfolds me
so that I can give love
bountifully.

The power of God protects me
and His hand guides me
carefully.

Where I am, God is!

Mama's Bible Story Book

As my mind wonders back so many years ago -
I think of our family gathered by the fireplace aglow.
Mama would take a book from the shelf
we loved almost as much as the Bible itself.
It was a children's Bible story book
and it taught us children how to look -
for God in all things good or bad.
Oh, the wonderful lessons that little book had!

When Mama read the exciting stories -
we could almost see heaven's glories.
How Moses and the Hebrews were fed -
with manna (God's own bread).
How Noah built an ark for animals two by two
because God told him just what to do.
Daniel who was in the lions' den,
And David who slew the biggest of men.
And Joshua who marched around -
and the walls of Jericho came down.

But the stories that we always wanted to hear -
were the ones of the Savior so dear.
The sweet Jesus who loves us so much,
and could make people well with His touch.
Jesus who died for our sin.
I still love to hear them over again.
Mama knew Jesus in a personal way -
and when she read the stories each day,
we couldn't help but want to know
this Savior that she loved so.

Years later in my life -
as a young mother and wife
I bought that same precious book, so -
that my children would learn to know -
the God who watches us all,
and answers when His name we call.

He That Built The House

He that built the house can restore it with love
    and might –
Only He can open the windows and let in the
    glorious sunlight –
He alone can tear down the walls that separate –
And build the walls that protect us from a
    dreadful fate.

Only the Great Builder alone –
Can set the foundation stone –
And take us back to that strong place –
To meet Him there face to face.

God alone can reach out with a loving hand,
And keep His house from sinking sand.

Prayer…
Dear God, we thank You for the restoration work You
are doing in Your house. We surrender it to You with
full confidence that You can not only build, but restore.

A New Ministering Spirit

"Ministering spirits are different from the angels,"
	Ann told me one day,
Sick and pale on her deathbed she lay.

"They have special ministries that they alone can do,
Because they are heavenly, yet have an earthly view.
That's the reason the Lord is calling me -
I believe with all my heart that's what I'm to be.
And the things that I seemingly left undone
Will be gloriously accomplished when the Lord and I
	are one.
So don't worry when my journey here ceases to be -
For at that very moment my ministering spirit will be
	totally free
And I can hardly wait to let the Lord use me."

A few days later, just as she said, her spirit laid down
	that body of clay
and was joyously on her way.
The thought holds such comfort and promise for me -
because - the Lord knew a ministering spirit is what
	she always wanted to be.

Matthew 18:18
*"Whatsoever ye bind in earth, shall be bound in heaven, and whatsoever
ye loose in earth shall be loosed in heaven."*

The Making of Angels

A man long ago –
visited the studio
of the famous Michelangelo.

After solemnly looking around –
a beautiful Angel statue he found.

Said he, "How do you do it?"
Michelangelo replied,
"There's really nothing to it."

Everything that doesn't look Angelic,
you chip away,
And just keep chipping until
it's an angel one day."

What a lesson we can learn
that when to the Master we turn –
He just keeps chipping our bad habits away –
Until we look like angels one day.

Ministering Angels

Sometimes the angels that God sends
come in the form of close friends.
You see God knows when you are lonely and blue,
So He sends a friend to minister to you.
sometimes all you need is an understanding smile,
or someone to talk to for a little while.

God is all-caring so He knows
which friend to send for our particular woes.
In sorrow they hold our hand,
in heartache they understand.
Happiness and joy they also share
because God really does care.

How thankful I am that He lovingly sends
His special angels in the form of friends.

The Garden Of Life

The garden of life is watered with tears,
Flowers grow from released fears.
Blossoms break forth from faith and love
That comes from God's light from above.

God Is Bigger Than My Mountain

There's a huge mountain in my life today –
It shadows my light and blocks my way.

The mountain is so big that it keeps me
from walking the path that God has for me.

It darkens my assurance that today the sun will shine.
It hinders the victory that I know is mine.

Even though in lieu of that mountain I feel
                                    hopeless and weak,
My Lord says in his Name to a mountain I can speak.
In my heart I know my God is bigger
                        than any mountain peak.

The Tree And Me

In the winter, Lord, the sap goes down deep in the tree
to prepare it for the cold winter that is to be.
It is left empty and experiencing hunger and thirst,
but if it were full of sap, when the freeze came,
                                    it would burst,
So the tree digs its roots deeper into the ground,
and its foundation becomes even more sound.

Lord, please teach me –
that I am like that old tree.
That there are times when we need to hunger and thirst,
so we can learn to seek you first.
When my roots get firmer in the ground,
only then will new joy be found.

Teach me, Lord, one other thing,
that after winter there always comes spring.

82

A Prayer

Lord, we come to You, bringing nothing but
    shipwrecked dreams, trouble and strife –
Born and carried in a worldly life.

Oh, how we wish we could bring riches of silver
    and gold to Your throne –
And rubies, emeralds, and diamonds to make
    them Your own.

But all we have are these tattered dreams
    from hearts that are sore –
Shattered hopes that only You, in Your love ,
    can restore

But, Lord, we bring this crumbled life to You,
    as at Your feet we bow –
Giving it all to You, and living for You in the
    here and now.

Just a Fingernail

As we discussed the Body of Christ, a glorious hope on
     her countenance fell –
"Oh, if the Lord would let me just be one little
     fingernail.
Just a fingernail to my Lord is loved and appreciated –
for each little part of His precious Body is valued and
     not hated.

We are all small parts, chosen of Him to make up the
     whole,
each tiny second given in love, bringing peace and joy
     to our soul."

How sweet to see a child of God, letting His humble
     Spirit prevail –
"Lord, I don't want to be important, just let me be a
     fingernail.
Let the finger that I am on point many to the truth
     and way
and the hand on which we are, comfort many today.
May the arm reach out to many and the shoulder help
     to bear
Another's heartaches, burdens and care.

May the neck spend time bowed in prayer, silently
     listening to the Head,
from whom the whole world is fed.
Oh, Lord, feed us all from Thy living well,
And thank you, Lord, for letting me be just a
     fingernail."

Romans 12:4
For as we have many members in one body, and all members have not the same office

The Old Place

The old house is still standing
Just as it was long ago
When her babies were small and demanding
And she baked her own bread, kneading the dough

Her chores were many
Her pleasures were few
She never had a penny
But she was never blue.

She found joy in simple living
Secure in her role
She was happiest when giving
Because God owned her soul.

She now has a mansion all her own
In Heaven with God's fold
She delights in happiness she's known
And walks the streets of gold.

But selfish creatures that we are
When we go back to the old home place
We long for days gone afar
And the smile of her lovely face.

Dear God,

I praise You that upon You – I can rest,
As I go through this trial and test,
For today in prayer – to me You've shown,
That a trial must present evidence that is known.
faith is the substance of things hoped for –
and evidence of things unseen.
So let me present that evidence unchanged,
        purified, and clean.

And then into my heart another truth you burned
That a test is just a sample – of things I have
        learned.
Lord, I have learned so much –
While waiting for Your healing touch.
And when the trial and test is over –
        let the world see
Your loving Holy Spirit alive and living in me.

Amen.

Live In A Landmark

Live in a landmark! The thought never occurred to me
when this old house we first came to see.
All we wanted was a nice place 'out'
a home in the country, with acres about.

But there you stood, old house, looking sad and alone
as if to say, "I need someone all my own
to spread a little paint, or fix a floor or two."
So without much thought, we bought you.

If walls could talk, what a tale you could tell
about the Doctor that climbed the stairwell.
With feet so large your steps scarce could hold
I'm sure your railing trembled under big hands so bold.

The left front room was a post office we're told...
In the attic we found records of stamps that were sold.
The right front room was the parlor, we know
where the family read by the fireplace aglow.

How many people visited, and over night slept
in the 'Preachers' Room" that was for company kept?
Where did they come from? Where did they go?
Old house, your secrets we would love to know.

Live in a Landmark! We're giving it a try.
And we've made some discoveries as days pass by.
A home whose history will last and last,
Gives us hope for the future and respect for the past.

Dear Lord,

I want to believe (and I know I should)
that all things work for good.
For those who love You
and are willing Your will to do.

But sometimes when my eyes are filled with tears
and when my heart aches with fears
When I know I need more faith in You
I find it is so very hard to do.

In Your word You promised me
that the good I'd see.
And one day I'd see the meaning clear
and never again have pain and fear.

Convicted as Charged

If I were arrested and charged for being a Christian,
        I hope there'd be,
enough evidence at my trial to convict me.

Would my holiness set me apart?
Could the officials see Christ living in my heart?

Would there be witnesses to swear –
that I carried God's love everywhere?

Would the Lord's light shine on my face
so they would know I have His grace?

Lord, let the proof be there for the world to see,
that I am a Christian and You live in me.

A Fresh Start

Lo, the winter is past –
The flowers appear on the earth.
At long last –
The earth breaks forth in new birth.

The trees that looked dead before –
now wear coats of green.
The grass that covers the earth's floor,
has a fragrance that is so clean.

Lord, let me not think of the past,
or things that might have been –
but let me at long last –
begin all over again.

Let this heart that was hard before
be fresh with new love –
Let my tongue sing of the Savior I adore –
and the glory be Thine above.

Be Still

The voices of nature are heard only when man is
    still
It is then we hear a bird's sweet song high upon a
    hill
We can hear the rivers flowing gently to the sea.
The drumming of the woodpecker and the buzzing
    of the bee.

Nature tells her secrets when we are quiet and
    still.
Her salty breath we taste and her soft breeze we
    feel.
A nut falls down from a large hickory tree.
A squirrel scampers away with it happily.

Lord, teach me to be very still.
And to search and listen for Your will.
For just like nature I want to be.
In the perfect place You have for me.

Psalm 46:10
"Be still, and know that I am God."

Keepers of The Springs

There was a town, long ago
that grew up at the foot of a mountain, so –
the people to a tradition wanted to cling
by getting their water from a mountain spring.

Up in the mountain there dwelled a man
who cleaned the spring by hand
keeping all foreign matter out of the way,
he worked diligently every day.

The town council one day met
and begin to argue and fret
over the monetary sum
of keeping the spring free of scum.

They decided to build a reservoir
for each man and woman, girl and boy.
Then calamity hit the town
and fever went around.

The keeper was called back once more
to do the job that he did before.
Soon the spring flowed clear
and from sickness there was no fear.

Women today are keepers of springs
they are the people who bring
goodness and purity to life
and clean out the dirt and strife.

In this world of sin and greed
there has never been a greater need
for 'keepers' with a gentle hand
to clean the filth in this land.

It's not an easy task – nor a popular one
but it is one that must be done.
For the sake of the children, young women today
must decide to do things God's way.

Or else what will be our country's fate?
Lower standards never made anything great.
If morality takes a lower tone,
then purity in our children is gone.

It is not progress when womanhood
gives up the opportunity to do good.
It is not progress when morals are pushed away
and ideals are forsaken for a modern day.

It is more noble to be a good mother and wife –
than to achieve great acclaim in life.
If we would be morally right instead of socially
correct
I wonder what would be the effect?

The school makes little effort, the church can't do
it alone
We must teach our children on our own.
with the help of God above –
We can do it with motherly love.

Inspired by a sermon by Dr. Peter Marshall.

A New Year's Story

'Twas the day before New Years and all through
    the house,
Not a commode was flushing and I smelled a dead
    mouse.
I woke Dad up early, with a list of to do's,
And gently suggested he put on his wading boots,
    not his shoes.
He asked no questions the stench was enough
"I'll put on my work clothes and get my plumbing
    stuff."
The clinch of his teeth and the set of his jaw...
Gave him a determined look that I never saw.
He spoke not a word, but went straight to his
    work...
Got his "plumber's friend" and turned with a jerk.
He put a clothes pin on his nose -
As the stench arose.
He went outside and got the plumber's snake -
as I prayed, Lord, let him fix it for all our sake.
Just in time as the guest arrived!
I heard the sound on which our marriage thrived.
One flush, then another, one or two...
It was going down, oh, thank goodness it's true.
But I heard him exclaim as he disappeared out of
    site
Happy New Year to all and to all a good night.

December 31, 1999

How To Make Lemonade

"When life hands you a lemon," the statement
has been made,
"Don't worry and fret, just make lemonade."
Though I know this statement is true –
No one ever mentions just what to do.

So I took my 'lemons' and considered them with strife,
Instead of a single lemon they had piled up in my life.

I took the first lemon and noticed its hard sheen –
And as I rolled it on my counter to soften it my hands
were cleaned.

A wonderful clean smell began to fill the air –
As I now began to soften it with tender care –
When it was all softened up
I squeezed the juice in my waiting cup.

"Water must be added," the Lord then said to me,
In My Word water stands for Spirit, are you beginning
to see?

Sugar sweetens this drink so tart –
Just as God's love sweetens a sour heart.

Lord, thank You for this insight divine –
And thank You that I know lemons are grown in
sunshine.

A Banana Puddin' Christian

A banana pudding Christian is what I
    sometimes want to be
Always asking God for the things that are
    smooth to me
Never thinking as I seek and pray
That His life is most times the rough way.

Never realizing that what might look good
    today
Could be a stumbling block tomorrow as I
    go on my way
Never thinking that He wants to add
    strength instead of fat
And His meaty Word will give me spice,
    instead of being vanilla and flat.

The Light Of Love

Lord, guide me with Your mighty hand.
Let my light shine in this perverse land.
when nothing but darkness surrounds,
and dark sin abounds.
Give me the grace so others can see,
the light of Your love living in me.

I wonder what could be
accomplished...
and remember that "I" said it...

If no one really cared about who
got the credit!!

CPSIA information can be obtained at www.ICGtesting.com
Printed in the USA
LVOW11s0118170914

404377LV00001B/72/P